ANTHONY

ANTHONY

A Play in Five Acts

by

Alexandre Dumas Père

Translated and Adapted by

Frank J. Morlock

The Borgo Press

An Imprint of Wildside Press LLC

MMIX

FIRST EDITION

CONTENTS

DEDICATION

To C. Conrad Cady

Who has encouraged and supported my efforts
To translate Dumas for many years, and
Has earned my sincere and deep gratitude.

INTRODUCTION

By 1831 Dumas was already an established play-wright, although his career as a novelist for which he is now remembered had not yet begun. *The Three Musketeers* would not even begin to appear until 1844.

In 1829 Dumas had scored a huge success with *Henry IV and his Court*. This was followed by Hugo's *Hernani* in 1830, and the Romantic Movement was in full swing. In 1831 Dumas brought forth *Anthony*, the only work for which he is still remembered as a dramatist. In *Anthony*, Dumas intended not only to vent some autobiographical material, but also to bring the Romantic hero out of history and into contemporary setting. This he proceeded to do with a challenge to society that has never been exceeded.

Anthony is the Romantic hero, not in armor, but in a top-coat. He is neither a poet nor a superman, but he is an outcast. And he has a lot of Dumas in him.

If under the Ancien Régime in France, birth mattered most, and under the Revolution, talent and will, then under the Restoration you needed both. It was no longer enough to be of high birth, you had to have talent and ambition to succeed. But just talent was not enough. That seems to be the message of Stendhal's *The Red and the Black*: Julien Sorel is loaded with talent, but has only a common peasant name. Julien chooses the Church where his low birth will not matter, but it seems it does, and his fate is tragic. You see similar struggles in some of Balzac's characters.

Anthony is described as wealthy and talented, but he's a bastard and cannot advance in a society that insists on a legitimate pedigree as well. If society closes its doors to him, why obey its laws? And Anthony is probably the wildest of all the heroes of the romantic period. He has no ambition to lead society or even enter into it, but he does demand the right to love and be loved no matter what. That love, no social convention will be allowed to obstruct. Society can shut him out, he doesn't care; but neither social conventions nor morality will keep him from being with his lover. It's about as uncompromising a defiance as I can think of in literature.

ANTHONY, BY ALEXANDRE DUMAS PÈRE

The only thing at all like it is a play called *Beirut*, written in the early days of the AIDS crisis, which asserts the right of lovers to be together, even if that means infecting the other with disease—and society's views be damned.

—Frank J. Morlock
October 2007

TRANSLATOR'S NOTE

As I edit this work for publication, I realize that my use of dashes is a little unorthodox, but in most cases I've retained them. French dramatists employ dashes or dots to indicate either a slight pause or in some cases a connection between ideas in a sort of stream of consciousness, where no equivalent English punctuation (such as a comma, colon, or semi-colon) actually conveys the same thought fully. This usage—which is in the original text—has been retained.

CAST OF CHARACTERS

Anthony

Adèle d'Hervey

Eugène d'Hervilly

Olivier Delaunay, a doctor

The Vicomtess de Lacy

Baron de Marsanne

Frederick de Lussan

Colonel d'Hervey

Madame deCamps

Clara, Adèle's sister

Hostess of a small inn near Strasbourg

Louis, Anthony's servant

Henry, Adèle's servant

A Servant of the Vicomtess de Lacy

Adèle's Chambermaid

ANTHONY, BY ALEXANDRE DUMAS PÈRE

ACT ONE

A fashionable salon in the Faubourg St. Honoré.

VICOMTESS: (to Adèle) Goodbye, dear friend. Take very good care of your health. We need you this fall—and you'll need to be fresh and gay—do you hear!

ADÈLE: Don't worry—I'll do my best for that. Goodbye! Clara, ring for a servant. Have someone bring the carriage for the Vicomtess.

VICOMTESS: Do you really hear? The country, goat's milk, and exercise on horseback—that's my prescription—goodbye, Clara.

(she leaves)

ADÈLE: (sitting back down) Do you know why the Vicomtess gives more orders than a doctor?

CLARA: Do you know why, just a year ago the Vicomtess talked only of war?

ADÈLE: You naughty girl!

CLARA: Yes—Colonel Armand left a year ago for the Algerian war. In his absence Doctor Olivier Delauney was presented to the Vicomtess. War and Medicine changed hands. And you know our dear Vicomtess is the exact duplicate of the man who has the luck to please her. In three months if a young and handsome lawyer should come along she'll be giving consultations, the way she was mapping battle plans, and the way she was prescribing a regimen to cure you.

ADÈLE: And how is it you know all this, pretty country girl—only arrived in Paris two weeks ago?

CLARA: Didn't I know her before I left Paris? And the Madame deCamps came yesterday when you weren't home—she provided me with a complete biography of the Vicomtess.

ADÈLE: Oh, how glad I am not to be found at home! That woman makes me ill with her constant slanders.

CLARA: (to a servant who enters)

SERVANT: A letter.

CLARA: For me or my sister?

(taking it)

SERVANT: For the baroness.

ADÈLE: Give it to me—it's undoubtedly from my husband.

CLARA: (giving the letter to Adèle) That's not his writing. Anyway the letter is posted in Paris—and the Colonel is in Strasbourg.

ADÈLE: (looking at it) God!

CLARA: What's the matter with you?

ADÈLE: I was hoping never to see this seal or this handwriting again.

(she sits down and worries the letter between her hands)

CLARA: Adèle—calm yourself. You're trembling all over—who's this letter from?

ADÈLE: Oh—it's from him—it's from him.

CLARA: From him?

ADÈLE: There's his motto—which I also took for mine—"Now and Forever."

CLARA: Anthony!

ADÈLE: Yes—Anthony's back and he writes me—he dares to write me.

CLARA: Perhaps under the title of old friend.

ADÈLE: I don't believe in friendship following love.

CLARA: But remember, Adèle, the manner in which he left as soon as Colonel d'Hervey asked for you in marriage—when he could have asked father himself, who would have given him justice? For you loved him! He could hope to win you. Young, seemingly rich—loved by you—but not at all—he left—only asking you to wait for two weeks. The time expired—and no one heard tell of him anymore—and three years passed without anyone knowing in what part of the world he'd placed his restless and adventurous character. If that's not proof of indifference it's at least proof of capriciousness.

ADÈLE: Anthony was neither—capricious nor indifferent. He loved me as much as a profound and proud heart can and if he left—it's doubtless because he had encountered obstacles that human will could not overcome—oh, if you had followed him as I have in the midst of society where he seemed an outsider—because he was so superior—if you had seen him sad and severe in the midst of these young fools—elegant nonentities—if in the midst of those joyous and sparkling looks which in the evenings surrounded us, you would have seen his eyes constantly fixed on you—staring and somber—you would have guessed that the love they expressed would not allow itself to be beaten by difficulties.

(a pause)

And then when he left you would have been the first to say—it's because it was impossible for him to stay.

CLARA: But perhaps after three years of absence—this love—

ADÈLE: Look how his hand shook when he wrote this address—

CLARA: Oh, as for me, I am sure we are only going to find a friend—quite sincere and devoted.

ADÈLE: In that case—open this letter for me—I don't dare.

CLARA: (reading) "Madame", you see: "Madame"—

ADÈLE: (passionately) He has never had the right to call me any other name.

CLARA: (reading) "Will Madame allow an old friend—who you have perhaps forgotten even as to his name, to lay his respectful homage at your feet? On returning to

Paris, and before leaving again soon allow one a person invoking the rights of a long-established friendship to present himself to you this noon? Deign"—etc., "Anthony."

ADÈLE: This noon—! It's eleven o'clock. He's going to come.

CLARA: Well—all I see in this letter is very cold, very controlled.

ADÈLE: And the motto?

CLARA: It was his before he knew you perhaps and he kept it. But you know it would only be from vanity—for him to tell you that he still loves you?

ADÈLE: (putting her hand on her heart) I feel it here.

CLARA: He announces his departure.

ADÈLE: And if we see each other he'll stay. Listen, I don't want to see him. I don't want to! Clara, my dear sister, my friend, it's not from you, who know how much I loved him—that I would try to hide a single emotion of my heart. Oh, no, I'm really sure, I don't love him anymore. D'Hervey is so good, so worthy of being loved—that I've nursed no regret over the past. But I mustn't see Anthony again. If I see him, if he speaks to me—if he looks at me—oh—there's a fascination in his eyes, a charm in his voice—oh, no, no—you were going to leave. I'm the one who's going to leave. You will receive him. You, Clara—you will tell him. I've kept all the feelings of a friend for him that if Colonel d'Hervey was here, it would be for me as for him, a real pleasure to receive him—but that in the absence of my husband—for me, or rather for the public—I beg him not to try to see me again—Let him leave—and all that a friend can do with prayers will accompany him. Let him leave, or if he stays, I will be the one who will leave—show him my daughter—tell him I love her passionately, that this child is my joy, my happiness, my life. He'll ask you if sometime I mentioned him to you.

CLARA: I will tell him the truth: Never.

ADÈLE: On the contrary, tell him, "Yes, sometimes." If you were to say no, he would believe that I loved him still, and that I was afraid of his memory.

CLARA: Don't worry—! You know how he listens to me. I promise to get him to agree to leave without seeing you again.

SERVANT: (to Clara) The carriage is ready, Madame.

ADÈLE: That's good. Goodbye, Clara—now, be nice to Anthony—soften him with words of friendship so he won't be bitter because of what I demand from him— and if he cries, don't tell me about it when I return. Bye.

CLARA: You're messing up. That's my hat.

ADÈLE: That's right. Don't forget what I told you.

(she leaves)

CLARA: Oh, no.

(to herself)

Poor Adèle. I really knew she wasn't happy. But isn't it wrong that that letter should make her so uneasy? Anyway, it's better she should avoid him.

(going to the balcony and speaking to her sister)

Take care, Adèle. Those horses frighten me. When will you be back?

ADÈLE: Why—not before evening.

CLARA: Fine. Goodbye.

(calling a servant)

Henry—keep everyone out except a stranger—Mr. Anthony—go.

(servant leaves)

What's that noise?

VOICES: (in the street) Stop! Stop!

CLARA: (going to the window) The carriage. My sister! My God! Oh—yes. Stop! Stop! In the name of heaven, stop! She's my sister!

(shouting in the street. Clara screams and collapses in a

chair)

Oh, mercy! Mercy! My God!

SERVANT: (coming in) Madame—don't be afraid. The horses have stopped. A young man threw himself in front of them—there is no more danger.

CLARA: Oh, thanks—my God!

(noise in the street)

SEVERAL VOICES: He's dead! No! Yes—Injured. Where shall we take him?

ADÈLE: (in the street) To my house! To my house!

CLARA: My sister's voice! Nothing's happened to her? My God! My knees are shaking—I cannot walk— Adèle.

(she tries to leave)

SERVANT: What's wrong, Madame?

CLARA: It's my sister, my sister—the carriage—oh, it's you.

ADÈLE: (entering—very pale) Clara—sister! Don't worry—I'm not injured!

(to a servant)

Run, find a doctor. Dr. Delauney is closest. Or rather stop first at the Vicomtess de Lacy's—he's probably there—place the injured man in there—in the vestibule.

(the servant leaves)

Clara! Clara! Do you know it's him—him—Anthony.

CLARA: Anthony! God!

ADÈLE: And who else but he would have dared to throw himself in front of two runaway horses?

CLARA: And why?

ADÈLE: Don't you understand? He was coming here, the poor thing! He must have had his face disfigured.

CLARA: But are you sure it's really him?

ADÈLE: Oh, I am sure of it. And didn't I have time to look at him while they were carrying him here? Haven't I had time to recognize him while they trampled him underfoot?

CLARA: Oh—

ADÈLE: Listen—go to him—or better—send someone—and if you still have any doubts, tell them to bring to me the papers he had on him so I'll know who he is because he's passed out, you see, passed out—perhaps dead. Hurry up, go, go! And give me news of him.

(Clara goes)

News of him! Oh, it's I who ought to go looking for it! It's I who ought to be there to read in the doctor's eyes whether he'll live or die! His heart should begin to beat again under my hands. My eyes ought to be the first he recognizes. Wasn't it for me? Wasn't it in saving my life—oh, my God. Oh, my God—there would have been strangers there—cold hearted, indifferent, who gawk at him. Oh, God—won't someone come to tell me whether he's dead or alive?

(to a servant who enters)

Well?

SERVANT: (giving her a billfold and a knife) For Madame.

ADÈLE: Give it here. How's he doing—has he opened his eyes?

SERVANT: Not yet—but Mr. Delauney, has just come and is with him.

ADÈLE: Fine. Tell him to come up so I will know from him personally—go.

(exit servant)

Suppose I was mistaken and it wasn't him.

(opening the billfold)

God! I did well—my portrait. If someone other than I had

opened this billfold—he kept my portrait as a souvenir! Poor Anthony. I'm not as pretty as this—go! In your thoughts, I was beautiful—I was happy—you will find me much changed. I've suffered so much!

(continuing to look)

A letter from me! The only one I ever wrote him.

(reading)

I told him I loved him. The wretch! The imprudent man. Suppose I were to take it back. It's the only proof—this is the only one. Doubtless he's reread it a thousand times. It's his treasure, his consolation. And I will plunder him of it—and when his eyes have hardly reopened—dying for me—he'll put his hand to his breast—it won't be the wound he's searching for, it will be this letter, and he won't find it. And it's I who will have stolen it from him. Oh—that would be horrifying. Anyway, as for me, haven't I kept his dagger—which I was always frightened to see him wear? I didn't know that his pommel served him as motto and seal. I clearly recognize him in these ideas of love and death constantly blended together. Anthony! I cannot resist it. I have to go and—see—for myself.

Ah, Doctor Olivier—come, come! Well?

OLIVIER: Reassure yourself, Madame, the accident, though serious, is not dangerous.

ADÈLE: Are you telling the truth?

OLIVIER: I answer for the injured. You, will you take my word? But you yourself—the fright, the shock—

ADÈLE: Has he come to?

OLIVIER: Not yet. But your pallor?

ADÈLE: Why did you leave him?

OLIVIER: One of my colleagues is with him. They told me you wanted some news. Then I thought you might need—

ADÈLE: Me? Me? It's really a question of me—but how is he now? What have you done?

OLIVIER: Medical terms might frighten you—perhaps—

ADÈLE: Oh, no, no—I have to know—you understand— he saved my life. It's quite simple.

OLIVIER: (somewhat astonished) Yes, without a doubt, Madame—well, the carriage beam striking him caused a bad contusion on the right side of his breast. The vio- lence of the blow led to fainting—I have operated to re- lease some excess blood and now sleep and tranquility will do the rest.

But he cannot remain in the vestibule surrounded by servants and the curious—I've ordered in your name that he be carried here.

ADÈLE: Here—is he too weak to be taken home?

OLIVIER: There wouldn't be any inconvenience in that, at least regarding the dressing on the wound—it wouldn't be disturbed—but I thought that the gratitude which you seem so sensible of needed to be expressed.

ADÈLE: Yes, certainly.

(low)

And if he starts to talk and mentions my name.

(aloud)

Yes, yes, without doubt, you've done well—but he needs to be alone doesn't he? You yourself will stay in another room for the sight of a stranger—

OLIVIER: Still—

ADÈLE: Ah, you did say the least emotion would be fatal to him—you did say that or at least I thought you did—didn't you?

OLIVIER: (watching her) Yes, Madame—I said it—it's necessary—but this precaution is not for me—for myself as a doctor.

ADÈLE: He's here—Listen, I beg you. Say he needs to be alone. Say that you order that no one stay by him.

(Clara enters with the servants carrying Anthony.)

ADÈLE: Put him on the sofa. Clara, Doctor Olivier says we must leave the patient alone—and that we all ought to leave—you see doctor, I am giving the example.

Clara, you keep Dr. Olivier company—as for me, I am going to give some orders.

(Adèle leaves.)

OLIVIER: (to Clara) Pardon me—I am just checking the pulse is beating again—

(They leave—Anthony remains alone. Then after a moment, a small door opens stealthily and Adèle enters with precaution.)

ADÈLE: Finally, he's alone—Anthony? This is how I ought to see him—pale, dying—. The last time I saw him—he was as near me—full of life—planning a future for the two of us—"Fifteen days apart", he said, "and then an eternal reunion—" And as he left, he pressed his hand to my heart—"See how it's beating," he said, "Well, it's from joy, it's from hope." He left and three years, minute by minute, day by day— elapsed—slowly—separated.

He's near me—as if it were then—it's really him— it's really me—nothing has changed in appearance— only his heart hardly beats—and our love is a crime.

Anthony!

(hiding her head in her hands)

(Anthony opens his eyes, sees a woman, watches her fixedly and gathers his thoughts.)

ANTHONY: Adèle?

ADÈLE: (letting her hands fall) Ah!

ANTHONY: Adèle!

(He tries to rise.)

ADÈLE: Oh—stay put, stay put—you're injured and the least movement, the least attempt—

ANTHONY: Ah, yes, I feel it, in coming to myself and finding you near me, I thought you had left yesterday and seeing you again today. What have I done in these three years that are past? Three years and not a single memory.

ADÈLE: Oh—don't speak.

ANTHONY: I remember now, I saw you again, pale, ter-rified—I heard your shouts, a carriage, horses—I threw myself in front of it—then everything vanished in a cloud of blood—and I hoped to be dead.

ADÈLE: You are not seriously injured, sir, and soon, I hope—

ANTHONY: "Sir"—oh—bad luck to me, for my memory is returning. "Sir" well, I too, I will say "Madame" I will unlearn the name Adèle for that of d'Hervey—Madame d'Hervey—and the misfortune of an entire life is contained in those two words.

ADÈLE: You need nursing Anthony, and I am going to call.

ANTHONY: Anthony is my name—mine—still the same. A thousand joyful memories are in that name. But Ma-dame d'Hervey.

ADÈLE: Anthony!

ANTHONY: Oh—say my name that way again and I will forget everything—Oh! Don't go away from me, my

God—come back, come back—so I can see you—I won't speak intimately to you, I will call you Madame—come, come—I beg you. Yes, it's really you—still beautiful—alive—as if for you alone life has no bitter memories. So you are happy, Madame?

ADÈLE: Yes, happy.

ANTHONY: Me too, Adèle, I am happy.

ADÈLE: You?

ANTHONY: Why not? Suspect the worse, but here's the trouble—when one has nothing to hope or fear from life—when our judgment is pronounced here as if we were damned—the heart ceases to bleed—it numbs itself in its sadness—and despair also has its calm, which, seen by happy folk, resembles joy—and then, Madame, misfortune, joy, despair, are not vain words, an assembly of letters, which represent an idea in our imagination and nothing more—which time destroys and reassembles to form others. Who then, seeing me, watching me smile at you as I am smiling at you this very moment would dare say "Anthony is not happy"?

ADÈLE: Leave me alone.

ANTHONY: (pursuing his thought) For there are men—were I to go in their midst, as if crushed by sorrows, fall on a public square, and display to their avid and gaping eyes the wound in my breast and the scars on my arms—they would say "Oh the poor fellow—he's suffering"—for then—to their vulgar eyes—all will be visible—blood and wounds—and they'll come close—and from pity for a suffering that perhaps may be theirs tomorrow, they will help me—except that, betrayed in my most divine hopes—blaspheming God, soul torn and heart bleeding, I shall go to roll in the midst of their crowd, saying to them, "Oh, my friends, pity for me, pity, I am really hurting—I am really badly off"—They would say—"He's a nut—a fool" and they'd go away laughing.

ADÈLE: (trying to disengage her hand) Allow me—

ANTHONY: And it's for this that God wanted man not to be able to hide the blood of his body under his clothes but permits him to hide the wounds of his soul behind a smile.

(pulling her hands)

Look me in the face, Adèle, we are happy—aren't we?

ADÈLE: Oh, calm down. Agitated as you are, how will they be able to carry you to your home?

ANTHONY: Carry me home? You're going to—Ah, yes I understand.

ADÈLE: You cannot stay here since your condition is no cause for worry—all my friends who know you, know you loved me—and as for myself—

ANTHONY: Oh—speak for the world, Madame—it's necessary for me to be dying for me to remain here. In convulsions of agony—I could shake your hand—Ah, my God! Adèle! Adèle!

ADÈLE: Oh, no—if there were the least danger—if the doctor wouldn't answer for you—I would risk my reputation—which is no longer mine—to protect you. I would have an excuse in the eyes of the world. But—

ANTHONY: (tearing off his dressing) An excuse is

needed, is it?

ADÈLE: God! Oh, the wretch. He's torn it off—the dressing—blood, my God, blood!

(ringing)

Help! The bleeding will stop—won't it? He's going pale—and his eyes are shut—

ANTHONY: (falling back in a faint on the sofa) And now I shall stay—right?

CURTAIN

ANTHONY, BY ALEXANDRE DUMAS PÈRE

ACT TWO

The same apartment as Act One.

(Adèle's head leaning on her hands)

CLARA: (entering) Adèle?

ADÈLE: Well?

CLARA: I left Anthony.

ADÈLE: Anthony, always Anthony! Well—what's he want from me?

CLARA: He's going today.

ADÈLE: He's already recovered his health?

CLARA: Yes, but he's so sad.

ADÈLE: My God.

CLARA: You've really been cruel to him. For the five days since he saved you, he's hardly seen you and always with Dr. Olivier. Perhaps you're right. Yes, it's a duty imposed by the titles of wife and mother. But Adèle, the poor thing is suffering so much. He has a right to complain. A stranger would have received more looks and more cares from you. Aren't you afraid that so much reserve will make him suspect it's for yourself you are afraid to see him again?

ADÈLE: To see him again? Oh, my God—where is the necessity to see him again? Oh—the two of you will ruin me and then, you too, you like the others will say— "Why did you see him again?" Clara, you who are so happy—with a husband who loves you and that you married for love and who's afraid to leave you alone to spend two weeks with me. I understand that my fears appear exaggerated to you. But as for me, alone with my daughter, isolated with my memories, among which is one that pursues me like a ghost—Oh, you don't know what it is to have loved and not to be with the man one loved—I see him everywhere in the midst of the world—see him, sad, pale, watching the dance—I flee this vision and I hear a voice buzzing in my ear.

It's his. I come home and right near my baby's cradle—my heart leaps and starts. And I tremble to return and see him. Thus far, yes, before God I have only this memory to reproach myself with.

Well, for several days now—that's what my life has come to—I feared him when he was absent. Now that he is here, that he is no longer a vision, it will indeed be he when I see him, it will be his voice that I will hear— Oh, Clara, save me! In your arms he won't dare take me. If it is permitted for our bad angel to render himself visible, Anthony is mine.

CLARA: Listen, and all your fears will soon cease. He's leaving Paris—only I repeat, he wants to see you again before that, to confide a secret to you—on which his honor depends—then he will go forever—he's sworn it on his honor.

ADÈLE: Well, no, no, he's not the one who must leave— I am the one. As for me, my place is with my husband.

He's my defender and master. He will protect me even from myself. I am going to throw myself at his feet—in his arms. I will tell him "A man loved me before I was yours. He's pursuing me. I no longer belong to myself. I am your treasure. I am only a woman—perhaps alone I wouldn't have strength to resist seduction. Here I am friend—defend me, defend me!"

CLARA: Adèle, consider. What will your husband say? Will he understand your exaggerated fears? What are you risking by staying a little longer? Well, then?

ADÈLE: And if the courage to leave should fail me? If when I call strength to my aide I find nothing in my heart but love, passion? His sophisms obliterate my remaining reason and then—oh, no, my resolution is taken—he's the only one who can save me. Clara, prepare everything for my departure.

CLARA: Well, let me come with you. I don't want you to leave by yourself.

ADÈLE: No, no—I'll leave my daughter with you. The trip is long and tiring. I shouldn't expose that child to it. Stay with her. It's 9:30. My carriage can be ready at eleven o'clock. Do it very secretly. Yes, now I will receive him, I am no longer afraid of him. Sister—friend, I confide myself to you—you will have to help save me. Oh, tell me I'm right.

CLARA: I will do what you wish.

ADÈLE: Good—leave me alone for now. Come back at eleven o'clock. I will know, seeing you, that everything is ready and you won't have to say anything to me. Not a sign, not a word—which might make him suspect. Oh, you don't know him.

CLARA: Everything will be ready. At 11:00?

ADÈLE: At 11:00. Now, I ask you nothing more than the time to write a few lines.

(Clara goes out.)

ADÈLE: (writing) "Sir, the obstinacy with which you pursue me, when every duty makes me avoid you, forces me to leave Paris, I shall depart taking with me the only feelings that time and absence cannot alter—those of true friendship. Adèle d'Hervey"

Oh God—let this be my last sacrifice. I still have enough strength—but who knows?

SERVANT: (entering) Mr. Anthony.

ADÈLE: (sealing the letter) One moment—Good! Let him enter.

(Anthony enters.)

ADÈLE: You wanted to see me before going away— Despite the need that I felt to express to you my gratitude, I've hesitated for a while to receive you, Mr. Anthony. You insisted and I didn't think it proper to refuse so small a favor to the man without whom I might never be able to see either my daughter or my husband.

ANTHONY: Yes, Madame, I know that it is for them alone that I preserved you. As far as this gratitude you feel, does what I have done really deserve it? Another, the first-comer would have taken my place—and if no one had come your way, the coachman would have stopped the horses or they would have calmed themselves. The carriage pole would have stopped in a wall as easily as in my breast—and the same result would have occurred. What do these causes matter? It's luck and luck alone of which you must complain and which I must thank.

ADÈLE: Luck—and why deprive me of the only feeling that I can have for you? Is that generous? I ask you.

ANTHONY: Ah, it's that luck seems, up to now, to have alone ruled my destiny. If you knew how many of the most important events in my life have had trifling causes!

A young man that I had never seen twice before escorted me to your father's home. I went there, I don't know why as I went everywhere—I met this young man in the Bois de Boulogne—we understood each other without speaking—a common friend passed by and made us acquainted.

Well, if this friend hadn't come or my horse taken another path, and I didn't meet him, he would never have escorted me to your father's home and the events which for the last three years have tormented my life would have happened differently. Five days ago, I wouldn't have come to see you, I wouldn't have stopped your horses, and in that moment, never having known me, you wouldn't be obligated to have a single feeling for me—except that of gratitude. If you don't call it luck—what then do you call this infinite succession of small events, which, taken together fill a life with sadness or joy and which in and of themselves, aren't worth either a tear or a smile?

ADÈLE: But Anthony—don't you believe there are misgivings of the soul—presentiments?

ANTHONY: Presentiments! And has it never happened to you, suddenly to learn of the death of a beloved friend and say to yourself—what was I doing when this part of my heart died? Ah, I was dressing for a ball or laughing in the midst of a party?

ADÈLE: Yes, it's terrible to think of. As a man who had never had feelings of weakness when taking leave of a friend for the first time says "Adieu". Didn't he mean to say to the beloved friend, "I'm no longer here to watch over you. So I commend you to God who watches over us all." That's what I feel each time I use that word in parting from a friend—such are the thousand thoughts that awakes in me. Are you also saying you were created by chance?

ANTHONY: Well, since a word, a single word awakes in you so many different thoughts, when you heard someone utter the name Anthony before—my name—in the midst of noble names—distinguished, well known, did this isolated name stimulate the thought of isolation? Didn't you say sometimes that name couldn't be the name of my father—of my family? Didn't you desire to know who was my family, who was my father?

ADÈLE: Never—I thought your father died during your infancy and I pitied you. I knew no more of your family than of you. Your entire family, for me, was contained in you. You were there. I called you, Anthony. What need had I to search for other names?

ANTHONY: And when casting your eyes on society, you see each man supporting himself in order to live on some kind of industry, to give in order to have the right to receive—didn't you ask yourself why, alone, amongst all others, I had neither rank which exempted me from a profession or a profession which conferred rank upon me?

ADÈLE: Never—you appeared to me born for all ranks— called to fill all professions. I didn't dare label a man who appeared to me capable of becoming everything.

ANTHONY: Well, Madame, chance destroyed whatever possibility there was before my birth, before I could do anything. And then when the day came that I knew myself, what would have been positive and real for another man, was for me but a dream and deception. Having no world of my own, I was obliged to create one. I needed other sorrows, other pleasures, and perhaps other crimes!

ADÈLE: And why then? Why that?

ANTHONY: Why that! You really want to know? And if, like the others you went—oh, no, no—you are good—Adèle—oh!

ADÈLE: They're ringing—Silence! A visitor—You aren't going away; tomorrow perhaps would be too soon.

ANTHONY: Oh—curse on the world which comes to pursue me even here.

SERVANT: (entering) The Vicomtess de Lacy—Dr. Delaunay.

ADÈLE: Oh—mercy—calm down—so they don't notice anything.

ANTHONY: Calm down—me? I am calm. Ah, it's the Vicomtess and the doctor—eh! What do you want me to talk to them about? The latest fashion? The play which is all the rage? Why all that interests me greatly.

(The doctor and the Vicomtess enter.)

VICOMTESS: Hello, dear friend—I learned through Doctor Olivier that you could be counted on to receive today—so I ran. Why, you know I am still trembling—you ran a real danger.

ADÈLE: Oh, yes—and but for Mr. Anthony's courage—

VICOMTESS: Ah—here's your savior? You recall, sir, we are old acquaintances. I had the pleasure of seeing you at Adèle's before her marriage. So under this double title receive the expression of my truly sincere gratitude.

(giving Anthony her hand)

Look, doctor, this gentleman is completely well, a little pale still, but his pulse is good. Do you know you've made a cure about which I am almost jealous?

ADÈLE: So, this gentleman is paying me his goodbye visit.

VICOMTESS: You are continuing your travels?

ANTHONY: Yes, Madame.

VICOMTESS: And where are you going?

ANTHONY: Oh, I don't know yet, myself. God protect me from having any set idea. Whenever I can, I prefer to let Chance do the thinking for me. A frivolity decides me—a caprice leads me on and as I change plans, as I see new faces, the rapidity of my course prevents the fatigue of liking or disliking—as no heart is gladdened when I arrive, so no heart is broken when I leave—it's probable that I will arrive like others, after a certain number of steps, at the end of a voyage whose purpose I am unaware of—without having discovered whether life's a buffoon's joke or a sublime creation.

OLIVIER: But what does your family say about this continual running about?

ANTHONY: My family? Ah, it is true. My family is used to it.

(to Adèle)

Isn't that so, Madame? You who know my family.

VICOMTESS: (in a low voice) But really, Adèle, I hope indeed that you are not insisting that he leave. Pathological treatments always leave great weakness and it would endanger him a lot. Oh, I've heard prodigious things. They tell me you didn't want to receive him during the entire course of his convalescence because he loved you in the past.

ADÈLE: Oh—silence!

VICOMTESS: Don't worry, there are a hundred topics of conversation, they talk about literature—as for me, I detest literature.

ADÈLE: (trying to speak gaily) Why, I am going to scold you, too. I saw you pass by my windows today and you didn't come in.

VICOMTESS: I was in too much of a hurry—in my capacity as lady of charity I was going to visit the Hospice for Foundlings. Hey! Why, I ought to have taken you. It would have distracted you for a moment.

ANTHONY: And as for me, I would have asked permission to accompany you. I would have been very interested in studying the effect produced on strangers by the sight of these unfortunates.

VICOMTESS: Oh! That is painful indeed—but then they take the greatest care for them, they treat them like other children.

ANTHONY: It's very generous of those who take care.

ADÈLE: How is it mothers can—?

ANTHONY: There are some—As for me, I know it.

ADÈLE: You?

VICOMTESS: Then, from time to time, rich people who don't have children, come to choose one there—and take it for their own.

ANTHONY: Yes, it's a bazaar, like any other.

ADÈLE: (feelingly) Oh, if I didn't have children—I would willingly adopt one of those orphans.

ANTHONY: Orphans! How good you are.

VICOMTESS: Well—you would be wrong. There, they spend their lives with people of their own type.

ADÈLE: Oh—don't speak to me of those unfortunates. It makes me ill.

ANTHONY: Eh, what do you care, Madame!

(to the Vicomtess)

On the contrary, speak about it.

(changing his manner)

You were saying that they were there with people of their own sort, and that, Madame, would be wrong?

VICOMTESS: Doubtless! Adoption cannot make you forget your true birth—and despite the education you would have given him, if he had been a man—what place could he occupy?

ANTHONY: Indeed—what would he become?

VICOMTESS: If she's a woman, how will she marry?

ANTHONY: Doubtless—who would marry an orphan? Me—perhaps, because I am above some prejudices— So, you see, the curse is pronounced; the wretched must remain wretched—for him God has no regard, and men, no pity. Without a name! Do you know what it is to be without a name? You would give it yours? Well yours, honorable as it is, would never take the place of a father's and by raising him from his obscurity and his nursery you wouldn't be able to give him what you snatched from him.

ADÈLE: Ah, if I knew a wretch like that, I would, in every way, with all kinds of attentions, make him forget that his position was sinful—for now, oh, now I understand.

VICOMTESS: Oh, and me, too.

ANTHONY: You too, Madame. And if one of those wretches were bold enough to love you?

ADÈLE: Oh, if I were free?

ANTHONY: That's not for you—it's for Madame.

VICOMTESS: He would understand, I hope, that his position—

ANTHONY: But suppose he forgot?

VICOMTESS: What woman would consent to love—?

ADÈLE: So in that situation—there remains—Only suicide?

VICOMTESS: Why—what's the matter with you? You are quite strange.

ANTHONY: Me? Nothing—I have a fever.

VICOMTESS: Come, come, don't go falling back in your access of misanthropy—oh, I'd forgotten your hate of men.

ANTHONY: Well, Madame, I am correcting myself. I hated them, you say? Since that time, I've seen much of them. Now, I only scorn them and for me to use a familiar term from the profession you affect now, it's an acute illness which has become chronic.

ADÈLE: But with these ideas you don't believe either in friendship or in—

(stops abruptly)

VICOMTESS: Well—"or in love"—

ANTHONY: (to the Vicomtess) In love, yes—in friendship, no—it's a bastard feeling that nature has no need for—a social convention that the heart adopts through egoism where the soul is constantly injured by the spirit, and that can be destroyed at once by the regard of a woman or the smile of a prince.

ADÈLE: Oh—you think so.

ANTHONY: Doubtless, ambition and love are passions. Friendship is only a feeling.

VICOMTESS: And with these principles, how many times have you loved?

ANTHONY: Ask the dead how many times they've lived.

VICOMTESS: Come, I see quite well that I'm being indiscreet. When you know me better, you will confide in me—from time to time I give soirees which my flatterers say are pleasant—if you stay, the doctor will bring you—or rather come yourself—I don't need to tell you that if your mother or your sister are in Paris, I will receive them with the same pleasure. Goodbye dear, Adèle—doctor will you come so I don't have to wait?

(to Adèle)

Well—he's better than when I knew him—much more gay—He must amuse you prodigiously. Goodbye. Goodbye—

(gives a last sign of her hand to Anthony, and leaves with the doctor)

ANTHONY: (after having bowed to her) Ill luck!

ADÈLE: (coming back) Anthony!

ANTHONY: Do you want me to tell you my secret now?

ADÈLE: Oh, I know it, I know it now. How that woman made me suffer!

ANTHONY: Suffer, bah! She's crazy—all that is only prejudice—and then I begin to find myself a little ridiculous.

ADÈLE: You?

ANTHONY: Surely! When I ought to live with people of my own kind, to have had the impudence to think that having a soul that feels, a head that thinks, a heart that beats—one has all that is needed to claim the place of man in society, his social rank in the world—vanity!

ADÈLE: Oh, I understand, now, all that remained obscure

to me—your somber character, which I thought fantastic—everything, everything—even your departure, which I couldn't account for! Poor Anthony!

ANTHONY: (beaten) Yes, poor Anthony! For who will tell you who could depict what I suffered when I was obliged to leave you? I had lost my unhappiness in your love: The days, the months stole, away like seconds, like thoughts; I forget everything near you—a man came and made me remember everything. He offered you rank, a name in society—and reminded me that I had neither rank nor a name to offer to the one to whom I would have offered my blood.

ADÈLE: And—why—why didn't you tell me that!

(looking at the clock)

Ten thirty—the wretch—the wretch!

ANTHONY: Tell you that! Yes, you who at the time thought to love me, would perhaps, have forgotten momentarily who I was—only to remember much later? But your parents, needed a name—and what likelihood was there they would prefer poor Anthony to the honorable Baron d'Hervey—it was then I asked you for two weeks—a last hope remained to me—there was a man charged, by I don't know whom, with giving me every year wherewithal to live for the year. I ran to find him. I threw myself at his feet, screams in my mouth, tears in my eyes. I adjured him by all he held most sacred— God, his soul, his mother—he—he had a mother, to tell me who were my parents—what I could hope or expect from them! A curse on him and may his mother die—I couldn't get anything out of him. I left like a madman, like one in despair ready to ask every woman, "You're not my mother, are you?"

ADÈLE: My friend!

ANTHONY: Other men, when events miss their hopes have a brother, a father a mother! Arms that open to them to come in and moan in. As for me—I don't have even a tombstone on which I can read a name and weep.

ADÈLE: Calm yourself, in the name of heaven, calm yourself.

ANTHONY: Other men have a country—I alone don't have one—for what's a country? A place where one is born, the family one leaves behind there, the friends one regrets there. As for me, I don't even know where I opened my eyes—I have no family, I have no country, everything for me was in a name—this name, it was yours and you forbid me to say it.

ADÈLE: Anthony, the world has its laws, society its demands—be they duties or prejudices, men have made them such and had I the wish to avoid them, still I would have to accept them.

ANTHONY: And why should I accept them? Not one of those who made them can boast of having spared me pain or done me a service. No, thanks to heaven, I've received only injustice from them and owe them hate. I will detest myself from the day when a man forces me to like him. Those to whom I have confided my secret have thrown in my face the fault of my mother. Poor mother! They said. "Bad luck to you who have no parents." Those from whom I've hidden it have slandered my life. They said "Shame on you who cannot reveal to society where your fortune comes to you from." Those two words—shame and misfortune are attached to me like two evil geniuses. I wanted to force prejudice to bow before education. Arts, languages, services, I've studied everything, understood everything—fool that I was to enlarge my heart so that despair could get in it. Natural gifts or acquired sciences all are effaced by the stain of my birth—careers open to the most mediocre men are closed to me; I have to say my name and I have no name—Oh would I were born poor and remained ignorant, lost amongst the populace—I would not have been pursued by prejudices; the closer they came to the earth, the more they diminish, until six feet below they disappear completely.

ADÈLE: Yes, yes, I understand. Oh, complain, complain,—for it's only with me you can complain.

ANTHONY: I saw you, I loved you, the dream of love succeeded that of ambition and science, I clung to life, I threw myself into the future, so rushed as I was, to forget the past—I was happy—a few days—the only ones in my life! Thanks angel! For it's to you I love this light of good, which I would not have known without you. Then it was that Colonel d'Hervey—Curse! Oh, if you knew how the misfortune makes me evil—how many times in thinking of this man I fall dozing—hand on my dagger. I dreamed of the graveyard and the scaffold.

ADÈLE: Anthony—you make me tremble.

ANTHONY: I left, I returned—there are three years between those two words. Those three years passed I don't know where or how—I wouldn't even be sure of having lived them, if I didn't have the memory of a vague and continual sadness. I don't fear the insults or the injustices of men—I felt only my heart, and my heart was entirely yours. I said to myself, "I will see her again—it is impossible that she has forgotten me—I will confess my secret to her—and then perhaps she will scorn me, hate me."

ADÈLE: Oh Anthony, how could you think that?

ANTHONY: And I, in my turn, will hate her as the others—or indeed when she learns what I've suffered, what I am suffering—perhaps she will allow me to remain near her—to live even in the same town as she lives.

ADÈLE: Impossible!

ANTHONY: Oh—I must have hate or love, Adèle! I insist on one or the other! I thought for a moment that I could go away again, fool that I was! I told you that but you must not believe it, Adèle. I love you, do you hear? If you want an ordinary love you must get yourself loved by a happy man—Duty and virtue—vain words— a murder will make you a widow—I can take it on my- self, this murder—let my blood spill over my own hand or that of any executioner—what does it matter?—it won't spill on anyone and won't stain the pavement. Ah, you thought you could love me, tell me so, show me heaven—and then break off everything with a few words said by a priest. Leave, flee, stay—you belong to me, Adèle—mine, you understand, I want you, I will have you—can there be a crime between you and me? So be it—I will commit it—Adèle, Adèle—I swear by this God that I blaspheme, by the mother I don't know!

ADÈLE: Calm yourself, wretch! You are threatening me—! You are threatening a woman.

ANTHONY: (throwing himself at her feet) Ah! Ah! Mercy! Mercy! Pity, help—do I know what I said—? My head is gone, my words are vain words with no sense—Oh, I am so unhappy—let me weep, let me weep—like a woman—oh, laugh—laugh—a man who weeps, right? I am laughing at myself, ah, ah—

ADÈLE: You are mad and you are driving me mad.

ANTHONY: Adèle! Adèle!

ADÈLE: Oh—look at the clock—it's going to strike eleven.

ANTHONY: Let it blot out one of my days and each of its minutes so long as I spend them near you.

ADÈLE: Oh—mercy! Mercy! In my turn Anthony—I don't have any more courage.

ANTHONY: One word! One word! Just one. And I will be your slave—I will obey at your gesture, were it to drive me away forever—one word, Adèle—years passed in hope of this word! If at this time you don't let this word of love escape your heart—When will I see you again?—When will I be as unhappy as I am—? Oh, if you don't have love for me, have pity for me.

ADÈLE: Anthony! Anthony!

ANTHONY: Close your eyes—forget the three years that are passed—only remember those moments of happiness when I was near you, when I said to you "Adèle, my angel—" and when you answered me, "Anthony! My Anthony! Yes, yes."

ADÈLE: (wildly) Anthony! My Anthony! Yes, yes, I love you.

ANTHONY: Oh—she is mine—I've got her back. I am happy.

(The clock strikes eleven.)

ADÈLE: Happy! Poor fool! Eleven o'clock! Eleven o'clock, and Clara is coming—he must leave us.

(Clara enters.)

ANTHONY: Oh, right now I much prefer to leave you than to see you in company.

ADÈLE: Be welcome, Clara.

ANTHONY: Oh—I'm going! Thanks—I bear away joy for eternity. Goodbye, Clara—my good Clara— Goodbye, Madame.

(low)

When will I see you again?

ADÈLE: Do I know?

ANTHONY: Tomorrow, right? Oh, tomorrow is so far off—

ADÈLE: Yes, tomorrow—soon—much too long.

ANTHONY: Forever! Goodbye.

(he leaves)

ADÈLE: (watching him and running to the door) Anthony.

CLARA: What are you doing? Courage! Courage!

ADÈLE: Oh—I have some—or rather I did, for it's all used up in my last words—oh, if you knew how he loves me—the madman!

CLARA: Did you prepare a letter for him?

ADÈLE: A letter? Yes, here it is.

CLARA: Give it to me.

ADÈLE: How cold this letter is—how cruelly cold—it will accuse me of falsity. Eh! Doesn't the world insist that I be false? This is what society calls duty, virtue. It's perfect, this letter. You will give it to him.

CLARA: Come, come everything is ready. The servant who is to accompany you—is waiting for you.

ADÈLE: Fine. Where must I go? Lead me—you can see indeed that I am ready to fall—that I haven't any strength, that I no longer can see.

(falling into a chair)

CLARA: Oh, sister—think of your husband.

ADÈLE: I no longer think of anyone except *him*.

CLARA: Think of your daughter.

ADÈLE: Ah, yes, my daughter.

(goes into the room)

CLARA: Embrace her—think of her—and now, now leave!

ADÈLE: (throwing herself into Clara's arm) Oh, Clara, Clara—how you must despise me! Don't go with me. I will speak to you of him again—goodbye, goodbye— take care of my daughter.

CLARA: Heaven protect you!

CURTAIN

ACT THREE

An inn at Ittenheim—two leagues from Strasbourg.

ANTHONY: (entering covered with dust, followed by a servant.)

(calling) Mistress of the inn?

HOSTESS: (coming from a nearby room) Here, sir—

ANTHONY: You are the mistress of this inn?

HOSTESS: Yes, sir—

ANTHONY: Fine—whereabouts are we—what's the name of this village?

HOSTESS: Ittenheim.

ANTHONY: How many leagues from here to Strasbourg?

HOSTESS: Two—

ANTHONY: Then there must be only two relay stations between here and Strasbourg.

HOSTESS: Yes, sir—

ANTHONY: (aside) I'm in time.

(aloud)

How many carriages have stopped here today?

HOSTESS: Only two.

ANTHONY: Describe the travelers.

HOSTESS: In the first there was an aged man with his family.

ANTHONY: In the other?

HOSTESS: A young man with his wife or sister.

ANTHONY: That's all?

HOSTESS: Yes, all.

ANTHONY: (to himself) Then it was indeed she that I met and passed about two leagues from this village as I left Vasselonne. In a half hour or three-quarters of an hour, she'll be here—that's well.

HOSTESS: Are you leaving, sir?

ANTHONY: No, I'm staying. How many post horses do you have in your stable?

HOSTESS: Four.

ANTHONY: And when you don't have any is it possible to procure any in the village?

HOSTESS: No, sir—

ANTHONY: I noticed as I entered in the shed an old four wheeler—is it yours?

HOSTESS: A traveler left it with us to sell.

ANTHONY: How much?

HOSTESS: Why—

ANTHONY: Hurry up, I don't have time.

HOSTESS: Twenty crowns.

ANTHONY: Here they are—anything lacking?

HOSTESS: No.

ANTHONY: How many vacant rooms in your inn?

HOSTESS: Two on the first floor.

ANTHONY: This one here?

HOSTESS: (opening the door) And this as well.

ANTHONY: I'll take them.

HOSTESS: Both of them?

ANTHONY: Yes—If a traveler was obliged to stay here tonight you could tell me—and perhaps—I would relinquish one.

HOSTESS: Do you have any other orders, sir?

ANTHONY: Hitch up—right, now you hear, right now—the four horses to the carriage I've just purchased so they'll be ready in five minutes.

HOSTESS: That's all?

ANTHONY: Yes, for the moment—anyway, I have my servant and if I need something I'll call you.

(the Hostess leaves)

ANTHONY: Louis.

LOUIS: (entering) Sir?

ANTHONY: You've served me for ten years?

LOUIS: Yes, sir.

ANTHONY: Have you ever had any complaint against me?

LOUIS: Never.

ANTHONY: Do you think you could find a better master?

LOUIS: No.

ANTHONY: Then you are devoted to me, right?

LOUIS: As much as one can be.

ANTHONY: You are going to get in the carriage they're hitching up and you're going to leave for Strasbourg.

LOUIS: Alone?

ANTHONY: Alone—you know Colonel d'Hervey?

LOUIS: Yes.

ANTHONY: You'll put on regular clothes and take lodgings facing his. You will join with his servants—if in a month, two months, three months, never mind when, you learn he's going to return to Paris you will leave for Paris as fast as you can to beat him there. If you learn he's already gone, overtake him—get ahead of him to warn me. You will have a hundred francs for each hour you are ahead of him—Here's my purse—when you have need of money, write me.

LOUIS: Is that all?

ANTHONY: No—you'll keep the coachman by making him drink so he doesn't get back with the horses until tomorrow morning—or at least until very late at night. Now—not an instant's delay—be vigilant—be faithful—leave!

(Louis leaves.)

ANTHONY: Ah, here I am alone, at last! Let's examine things—these two rooms communicate with each other. Yes, but on each side the door can be locked from within. Hell! This cabinet? No outlet. Suppose I removed this bolt? She might see it. This window? Ah, the balcony services both windows.

(he laughs)

A veritable terrace. Ah, that's fine. I am worn out.

(sits down)

Oh, how she deceived me! I didn't think she could be so false! Poor dope, to trust in her smile, in her tender voice for a moment. Like a fool, you were taken in with joy, and mistook a flash of light for the daylight! Poor dope, who did not know how to read in a smile, or detect in a voice and who, holding her in your arms, didn't choke her for belonging to someone else.

(rising)

And if she were to arrive here before Louis, whom she knows, leaves with the horses. Misfortune! No—I don't see the carriage anymore.

(sits down)

She's coming, congratulating herself on having deceived me, and in her husband's arms she will tell him everything—she will tell him that I was at her feet—forgetting my manhood—and groveling. She will tell him she repulsed me—then between kisses they will laugh over the fool, Anthony. Anthony, the bastard.

Laugh together! A thousand devils!

(striking the table with his dagger so that the blade almost entirely disappears)

(laughing)

The blade of this dagger is good.

(rising and running to the window)

Louis has finally gone. Now let her come. Marshall all the faculties of your being to love, create a hope of joy which devours all others, then come, soul tortured, eyes in tears, and kneel before a woman—this is all you get! Scorn and derision! Oh, if I were to go mad before she arrives. My thoughts clash in confusion—head is burning—where's there some marble in which to rest my face—? And when I think that all that is necessary to quit the hell of this life, is a moments' resolution, that the excitement of frenzy can succeed in a moment to the peace of nothingness—that nothing—not even the power of God can prevent it—if I wish it—why don't I wish it then?

Is it a word that stops me? Suicide! Surely when God made men—a lottery to the profit of death, and didn't give each man the same strength to support a quantity of sorrows—he must have realized that this man would succumb under the burden—that the weight would exceed his strength.

And where do these wretches came from who cannot return evil for evil? It is not fair and God is not just. Then so be it—let her suffer and weep as I have wept and suffered! She—weep! She suffer! Oh my God—she—my life—my soul—that's frightful! Oh, if she weeps let it be for my death at least. Anthony mourned by Adèle. Yes, but tears will be succeeded by melancholy, sadness indifference. Her heart will mend itself again from time to time—

When by chance my name is mentioned before her—then they won't mention it anymore. Forgetfulness will come—oblivion the second shroud of the dead! At last, she will be happy—but not alone. Someone else will share her happiness. This someone else—in two hours she'll be with him. For her whole life—and as for me—for my entire life—I will be far away—Ah—if he were never to see her again! Ah—didn't I hear something?

Yes, yes—the rolling of a carriage. Fortunately,

night is coming on. That carriage, it's hers. Oh, this time, I'll throw myself before you again, Adèle. But that won't save you. Five days without seeing me and she leaves me the day she sees me—and if the carriage had broken me in pieces against a wall, she'd have left the mutilated body at the door for fear that by taking the body into her home, she'd have compromised herself—come, come, Adèle! For you are loved, and you are waited for—here she is. From this window, I can see her. But do I know, seeing her, what I will do?

Oh, my heart, my heart—She's getting down—it's her voice, her sweet, sweet voice, which said yesterday, "till tomorrow, tomorrow, my friend." Tomorrow has come—and I am at the rendezvous—they're coming up—it's the hostess.

(sits, with apparent tranquility, on furniture near the door)

HOSTESS: (entering with two torches in hand—she places one on the table) Sir, a lady forced to stop here has need of a room. You were good enough to tell me you would relinquish one of those you retained. If you are still in the same mood, I beg you to tell me which of the two you will dispose in my favor.

ANTHONY: (with an air of indifference) Why it seems to me this one is the largest and most comfortable—I will be content with the other one.

HOSTESS: When, sir?

ANTHONY: Right now.

(the Hostess takes the second torch into the adjourning room and returns right away)

The lady will be at home here.

HOSTESS: I thank you, sir.

(she goes into the stairway door)

Madame! Madame! You can come up. This way. There.

ANTHONY: (going into the other room) There she is.

(Locks the door at the moment.)

(Adèle appears.)

ADÈLE: And you say it is impossible to procure any horses?

HOSTESS: Madame, the four horses left not a quarter of an hour ago.

ADÈLE: And when will they return?

HOSTESS: Tonight.

ADÈLE: Oh, my God—the very moment I arrived. When it's no more than two leagues to Strasbourg. Oh, see if there is not some way?

HOSTESS: I don't know of any—Ah, if the coachman who brought you is still below, perhaps he'll agree to drive on without changing horses.

ADÈLE: Yes, yes—that's a way. Run, tell him I'll give him whatever he asks—

(the hostess leaves)

Oh—he'll still be there—he'll agree—and in an hour I'll be with my husband. Oh, my God, I don't hear anything—I don't see anything—the coachman has left perhaps?

(Hostess returns)

Well?

HOSTESS: He's no longer here. The stranger who's relinquished this room to you spoke a few words to him from his window and he left immediately.

ADÈLE: How miserable I am!

HOSTESS: You seem really agitated.

ADÈLE: Yes, one more time. There's no way of leaving before the return of the horses?

HOSTESS: None, Madame.

ADÈLE: Leave me alone then, I beg you.

HOSTESS: If you need something, just ring.

(The Hostess leaves.)

84

ADÈLE: How does it come about that I am almost happy for this delay? Oh, it's that as I get closer to my husband, it seems to me I hear his voice, see his stern countenance.

What will I tell him of the motive of my flight?

That I am afraid of loving another? That fear alone, in the eyes of society, in his eyes—is almost a crime. If I told him the only desire was to see him? Ah, that would be deceiving him. Perhaps, I left too soon and the danger wasn't as great as I thought—oh, having seen him again, I wasn't happy, but at least I was calm—each tomorrow will resemble the day before. God, why this agitation, this trouble—when I see so many women—

Oh, it's because they are not loved by Anthony. The banal love of all other men made me smile from pity. But his love is uniquely his, his love—ah, to be loved so, and to be able to confess it to God and to the world—to be the religion, the idol, the life of a man like him—so superior to other men—to give him all the happiness I owe him—and the numberless days will pass like hours. Ah, still what a prejudice has carried me away—behold this just society which punishes in us a sin that neither one of us has committed. And in exchange, what has it given me? Ah, this will make me suspect celestial goodness. God—what did I hear?

Noise in that room. It's a stranger, a man I don't know who inhabits it. This room.

(she runs towards the door and slips the bolt in)

And I have forgotten. Why am I trembling like this?

(she rings)

Horses! Horses! In the name of God—I am dying here!

(at the stairway door)

Someone! Madame!

HOSTESS: (outside) I'm here, I am here.

(entering)

Madame is calling?

ADÈLE: I want to leave—have the horses returned?

HOSTESS: They hardly left when you arrived and I don't

expect them back for two or three hours. You ought to get some rest.

ADÈLE: Where?

HOSTESS: There's a bed in this closet.

ADÈLE: This closet doesn't lock.

HOSTESS: The two doors of this room lock from inside.

ADÈLE: That's true. I can be without fear here, right?

HOSTESS: (taking the torch into the closet) What could you fear, Madame?

ADÈLE: Nothing—I am crazy.

(the hostess comes out of the cabinet)

In the name of heaven! Warn me as soon as the horses return.

HOSTESS: As soon as they do, Madame.

ADÈLE: (entering the closet) Nothing's ever happened by accident in this hotel?

HOSTESS: Never—If you like, I will have some one watch.

ADÈLE: (entering the closet) No—no, indeed—Pardon— leave me.

(she goes into the cabinet and closes the door. Anthony appears on the balcony—behind the window—breaks a pane—puts his arm through, opening the window fastener, enters quickly and goes to the door the hostess left by and bolts it.)

ADÈLE: (coming out of the closet) Some noise—a man—oh!

ANTHONY: Silence.

(taking her in his arms and placing a handkerchief in her mouth)

It is I, I, Anthony.

(Dragging her into the closet.)

CURTAIN

ANTHONY, BY ALEXANDRE DUMAS PÈRE

ACT FOUR

A boudoir at the home of Vicomtess de Lacy—in the back, an open door, opening on an elegant salon prepared for a ball. To the left, a door in a corner.

VICOMTESS: (to several servants) Go—and don't forget anything I've told you. The most boring thing—to be mistress in your house alone. I've hardly had time to finish my toilette, and if this excellent Eugène hadn't helped me with my invitations I don't know how I'd get myself out of it—but he promised to be the first to get here.

SERVANT: (announcing) Mr. Eugène d'Hervilly.

VICOMTESS: (bowing) Sir.

EUGÈNE: (returning her bow) Madame.

(The servant leaves.)

VICOMTESS: (changing her manners) Ah—there you are—

(adjusting her hair with one hand, while giving him the other to kiss)

You are charming and precise enough to do honor to a mathematician. That's nice for a poet.

EUGÈNE: There are situations in which precision is not a very surprising virtue.

VICOMTESS: Really? So much the better. Do you like my hair do?

EUGÈNE: Charming.

VICOMTESS: Flatterer! Recognize this dress?

EUGÈNE: This dress?

VICOMTESS: Forgetful! That's the one I had on the first time I saw you.

EUGÈNE: Ah, yes—at— (trying to recall)

VICOMTESS: (impatiently) Madame Amédée deVals—only women have this sort of memory—That ought to be the best day, the greatest day of your life—do you remember the woman who didn't take her eyes off us?

EUGÈNE: Yes, Madame deCamps. That prude! Whose feet always got in the way and who, when one made excuses, seemed not to understand and replied "Yes, sir" for the first quadrille.

VICOMTESS: By the way I saw her after you left me and I argued with her. Argued until I was hoarse, about literature—you know I never talk about literature. It's really a way of compromising myself. It's your fault now. If you return in love all that I am risking for you at least—

EUGÈNE: What! Don't I love you the way you want to be loved?

VICOMTESS: He asks that! When I saw a poet was occupying himself with me, I was enchanted, I said to myself—"Oh, I am going to find an ardent soul, an impassioned mind full of new and profound emotions." Not at all! You loved me as if you were a stockbroker.

Would you tell me where you've hidden those fiery scenes you've put on in the theater? For you won't succeed in confusing me—for it's there your plays succeed—and not in the history, the manners, the local color—what do I know? Oh, I'm furious with you—mortally furious for having deceived me, yet I am laughing about it.

EUGÈNE: Listen, as for me, I too, Madame, was seeking everywhere this delirium of love of which you speak. I too, I asked it of every woman—ten times I was on the point of obtaining it from them—but for some I didn't tie my tie well enough, for others I leapt too much in dancing the waltz. The last one was going to love me to adoration when she noticed I don't dance the gallop. In short, it always escaped me the moment I felt sure I'd inspired it.

That's the dream of the soul so long as it is young and naive. The whole world has that dream. Only to see it faint slowly, I began like others and finished like them.

I accepted life as it came and I held it quits of what it had promised—I've spent five or six years looking for this ideal love in the midst of our elegant and gay society. I ended my research with the word "impossible."

VICOMTESS: Impossible! Look how Anthony loves. That's the way I would have wanted to be loved.

EUGÈNE: Oh that's another matter—take care Madame—a love like Anthony's would kill you. From the moment that you didn't find him ridiculous. You are not, like Madame d'Hervey a woman with pale complexion, sad eyes, a severe mouth. Your complexion is rosy, your eyes are sparkling, your mouth is gay—violent passions will destroy all that and that would be a shame—you surrounded by flowers and silk gauze. You want to love and be loved with passion? Ah, beware, Madame.

VICOMTESS: Why—you frighten me! Indeed, perhaps it would be better just as it is.

EUGÈNE: (gaily) Oh without doubt. You order a dress—you tell me you love me. You go to a ball. You return with a headache, time passes—your heart remains free—your head is crazy and if you have something to complain of it's that life is so short, and some days are so long.

VICOMTESS: Silence, madman that you are! Everybody's coming.

SERVANT: Madame deCamps.

VICOMTESS: Your antipathy.

EUGÈNE: I admit it. Prudish and malicious.

VICOMTESS: Hush.

(to Madame deCamps)

Ah, come in.

MME deCAMPS: I've come early, dear Marie, it's embarrassing for a widow to present herself alone in the midst of a ball. You feel everyone is staring at you.

VICOMTESS: Why, it seems to me it's a misfortune to

be feared less than all others.

MME deCAMPS: You are flattering me. Are you still mad at me over our little literary dispute?

(to Eugène)

You're the one who is turning her into a romantic, sir, it's a sin for which you will have to answer on judgment day.

EUGÈNE: I don't know, Madame, by what influence I could.

MME deCAMPS: Oh—neither do I. But the fact is she no longer says a word about medicine, and all the medical professors and Dr. Delaunay have been completely abandoned for Shakespeare, Schiller, Goethe, and you.

VICOMTESS: Wicked thing that you are, you are going to give people ideas.

MME deCAMPS: Oh—it's only a joke. And who will we have to our beautiful soiree? All Paris?

VICOMTESS: At first—then our usual friends; some presentations of young people who dance—that's precious, the type is becoming more rare day by day. Ah—Adèle d'Hervey who's returning to society.

MME deCAMPS: Yes, she deserted us under the pretext of bad health for thee months—after the adventure in the inn—what I do know! Really, darling Marie, are you inviting that woman? Well, you're wrong—don't you know?

VICOMTESS: I know that they say thousands of things that are untrue—probably. But Adèle is an old friend of mine.

MME deCAMPS: Oh—I'm not reproaching you. You are so good—you've only seen in this invitation a way of rehabilitating her, but it's for her to understand she's lost standing in a certain world, and if she doesn't understand that—it would be charity to make her realize it. If her adventure had not made such a sensation. But why was her sister in such a hurry to say she left to rejoin her husband? Then a few days later—she was seen to return. Mr. Anthony, absent with her, returns at the same time as she—Doubtless you also invited Mr. Anthony.

VICOMTESS: Certainly!

MME deCAMPS: I'll be enchanted to see Mr. Anthony. I love puzzles.

VICOMTESS: What?

MME deCAMPS: Doubtless—isn't this a puzzle?—living in the midst of society as a rich man whose family and situation no one knows. As for me, I don't know of any profession that doesn't require a family and a situation.

EUGÈNE: Ah, Madame!

MME deCAMPS: Doubtless! Nothing as dramatic as a mystery in a theater or a novel—except in society.

SERVANT: (announcing) Baron de Marsanne, Mr. Frederick de Lussan, Mr. Darcey.

(they enter along with others whose names are not spoken)

VICOMTESS: (to the Baron) Ah, it's very sweet of you, Baron.

(familiarly to Frederick)

You are a charming man. You're going to dance, right?

FREDERICK: Why Madame, I shall be at your orders, today as always.

VICOMTESS: Pay attention! I have witnesses—Mr. Darcey, I promised you to these ladies.

(to a young girl who enters with her mother)

Oh, how pretty you are! Come here my beautiful angel.

(to the mother)

You will leave her to us, right—later—much later.

MOTHER: But Vicomtess.

VICOMTESS: I have three people who need you for cards.

SERVANT: Dr. Olivier Delaunay.

(The women smile and look alternatively from Eugène to Olivier.)

OLIVIER: Madame.

VICOMTESS: Hello, Doctor—I am enchanted to see you—you will find Mr. Anthony here tonight, I presumed it would be agreeable to you to meet him. That's why my invitation was so pressing.

FREDERICK: (going to Olivier) Why I was looking everywhere for you when I came. I was expecting that the honors of the house given me were really for you.

OLIVIER: (noticing Eugène who comes to them) Hush!

FREDERICK: Bah!

OLIVIER: Word of honor!

EUGÈNE: Hello, Doctor.

OLIVIER: Well, my friend, successful plays?

EUGÈNE: Well, my dear boy, sick patients?

OLIVIER: Do they still hiss?

EUGÈNE: Do they sometimes die?

SERVANT: The Baroness d'Hervey.

MME deCAMPS: (to the women surrounding her) The heroine of the adventure I was telling you about.

(Adèle enters.)

VICOMTESS: Hello, dear Adèle. Well, didn't you bring your sister, Clara?

ADÈLE: She left a few days ago to rejoin her husband.

MME deCAMPS: Why, we'll probably see her again soon. Those trips are not usually of long duration.

VICOMTESS: (excitedly to Adèle) Dear friend, allow me to present to you Mr. Eugène d'Her-villy—who you know, by name, without a doubt.

ADÈLE: Oh, sir, I am really unworthy—for three months I've been ill—I hardly go out from pain and consequently I haven't been able to see your latest work.

VICOMTESS: Blasphemer! Get out. And quickly. I will send you my box—the first time they play it—

(to Eugène)

You'll remind me.

SERVANT: Mr. Anthony.

(everyone turns. Eyes switched from Adèle to Anthony as he enters. Anthony bows to the Vicomtess, then the ladies en masse—Olivier goes to him, they talk. Eugène watches him with curiosity and interest)

ADÈLE: (to hide her trouble quickly turns to Eugène) And doubtless you are finishing something, sir?

EUGÈNE: Yes, Madame.

MME deCAMPS: Still about the Middle Ages?

EUGÈNE: Still.

VICOMTESS: It's what I tell him all the time. "Create something relevant." Isn't everyone more interested in people of our time, dressed like us, speaking the same language?

BARON DE MARSANNE: Oh, it's because it's really much more easy to find a topic in history than in imagination. You can find plays there almost written.

FREDERICK: Yes, almost.

BARON DE MARSANNE: Hell! See what the papers say about—

EUGÈNE: Several discussions, much too long to develop, but not to prevent me doing it—

VICOMTESS: Advance your reasons and we will judge.

EUGÈNE: Oh, ladies, allow me to tell you this would be a course much too serious for an audience in ball gown and party finery.

MME deCAMPS: Why, not at all. You see no one is dancing yet—and besides we are all interested in literature, aren't we, Vicomtess?

BARON DE MARSANNE: Patience ladies, the author will reveal all his ideas in the preface of his next work.

VICOMTESS: Are you writing a preface?

BARON DE MARSANNE: The Romantics are all for prefaces. The papers were joking about it the other day so cleverly.

ADÈLE: You see, sir, you are employed to defend yourself, a time that would have sufficed to develop a complete system.

EUGÈNE: And you, too, Madame, pay attention—you insisted on it, I am not responsible for boring you—here are my themes—comedy is the pantomiming of manners—drama that of passions-- the Revolution as it passed over France rendered all men equal, confused ranks, generalized wearing apparel. Nothing indicates the profession. No club can shut out such manners or habits, everything's mixed together. Manners have replaced colors, and it's necessary to have colors and not nuances to a painter who wants to create a scene.

ADÈLE: That's true.

BARON DE MARSANNE: Still, sir—the papers—

EUGÈNE: (without listening) I was saying that the comedy of manners become in this way, if not impossible at least very difficult to render. There remains the drama of passion and here another difficulty presents itself. History bequeaths us some facts, they belong to us by right of inheritance, they are incontestable; they are poetic. It exhumes men of past times, it reclothes them in their costumes, agitates their passions, which it augments or diminishes according to whatever dramatic point it wants to reach. But when we try, in the midst of our modern society, under our stiff cutaway evening clothes—to show the naked heart of man—it won't be recognized. The resemblance between the hero and the audience would be too close—the analogy very intimate, the spectator who follows the actor in the development of the passion wants to stop him at the point he would himself have stopped—if it surpasses his ability to feel or express, he doesn't grasp it, he will say—

"This is false. I don't feel that way—when the woman I love hates me, doubtless I suffer—yes—sometimes but I don't stab her, nor kill her and the proof is—here I am".

Then the shouts of exaggeration cover the applause of some men who, more happily or more unhappily constituted than the others, feel that the passions are the same in the nineteenth century as in the fifteenth century and that the heart beats with blood just as hot under a top-coat or a steel suit of armor.

ADÈLE: Well, sir, the approval of some men will compensate you amply for the coldness of others.

MME deCAMPS: Then should they doubt it, you could give them proof that the passions truly exist in our society. There are still profound amours that a three year absence cannot extinguish, mysterious cavaliers who save the life of the women of their thoughts—virtuous women who flee their lover, and as the mixing of nature and the sublime is fashionable have scenes which are not less dramatic for taking place in a room in an inn. I will depict one of these women.

ANTHONY: (who has said nothing during the entire literary discussion, but whose face has become increasingly agitated, and leaning over the back of Mme deCamps's armchair) You by chance have a brother or a husband?

MME deCAMPS: (astonished) What does that matter to you, sir?

ANTHONY: I need to know!

MME deCAMPS: No!

ANTHONY: Well, then shame rather than bloodshed.

(to Eugène)

Yes, the lady's right, sir, and since she's made it her business to trace the subject to its depths, I shall make it my business, too, to furnish you the details. Yes, I will take this pure and innocent woman—more than all women—and I will show her loving and candid heart, scorned by this corrupt society, at heart worn out and corrupt. I put in opposition to her one of those women whom all morality would approve—who wouldn't flee the danger because she's long been familiar with it, who will abuse her woman's weakness—to kill in a cowardly way that woman's reputation as a woman, just as a bully abuses his strength to kill the existence of a man. I will prove that the first of the two to be compromised will be the honest woman, and that, not from a fault of virtue but from lacking practice—Then in the face of society, I will demand justice between them here below, while waiting for God to render it on high.

(Silence for a moment.)

ANTHONY: Come ladies, that's long enough to discuss literature—music calls you for the quadrille.

EUGÈNE: (gallantly offering his hand to Adèle) Madame, may I have the honor—?

ADÈLE: I thank you, sir—I don't dance.

(Anthony takes Eugène's hand and shakes it.)

MME deCAMPS: Goodbye, dear Vicomtess.

VICOMTESS: What—you are going?

MME deCAMPS: (as she leaves) I cannot remain after such a frightful scene.

VICOMTESS: (following her) You provoked it a little, you must agree.

(Adèle remains alone. Anthony watches her to know if he is to stay or leave. She gestures for him to leave.)

ADÈLE: Ah, why did I come, My God? I suspected as much. Everything is known—not everything—but soon—everything.

Ruined! Ruined forever! What to do? Leave. All eyes will be fixed on me. Remain—all voices will cry out at the impudence. Still, I really was ill for three months. That ought to be some expiation.

VICOMTESS: (entering) Well—Ah! I was looking for you, Adèle.

ADÈLE: How good you are!

VICOMTESS: And you—how crazy you are. Good God! I thought you would start crying.

ADÈLE: Oh—do you think there's no reason to?

VICOMTESS: For a word?

ADÈLE: A word that kills.

VICOMTESS: Why that woman would ruin twenty reputations a day if anyone believed her.

ADÈLE: (rising with excitement) No one believes her, do they? You don't believe her, do you? Thanks! Thanks!

VICOMTESS: But you yourself dear Adèle, must learn how to control your face a little.

ADÈLE: How and why would I have learned it? Oh, I don't know how, I'll never know how.

VICOMTESS: But if, child, I spoke like you? In the midst of this society—one hears a crowd of things which ought to slide by without touching or if they do touch, well, a calm look, an indifferent smile.

ADÈLE: Oh, that's what is frightful, Marie, it's that you yourself already thought this of me, that a day will come when I will greet the insult or not recoil before the scorn, when I will look before me, with a calm expression, and indifferent smile as my reputation as a wife and mother, like a child's toy, passes between hands which will destroy it. Oh, my heart! My heart. Rather they torture it, tear it apart—my God! Marie, you know up till now, it was pure, if any voice in society had dared to—touch—

VICOMTESS: Well, but that's precisely what they won't forgive you—right or wrong, a woman must atone one day—but what do you care if your conscience is clear?

ADÈLE: Yes, if my conscience is clear—

VICOMTESS: If when you go home, alone with yourself, you can smile as you see yourself in the mirror and say "slander"—if your friends continue to see you—

ADÈLE: From respect for my rank, my social position.

VICOMTESS: If they offer you their hand—hug you—look—

ADÈLE: From pity perhaps, from pity—and it's a

woman, who playing a smile on her lips, lets fall on another woman a word of dishonor—accompanying it with a sweet and affectionate look to know if it penetrated the heart and if it drew blood—infamy! But have I ever done anything to that woman?

VICOMTESS: Adèle!

ADÈLE: She's going to go repeat this everywhere. She will say I didn't dare to look her in the face, and that she made me blush and cry—oh, this time, she'll speak the truth for I am blushing and crying.

VICOMTESS: Oh, my God—calm down; and I who must leave you.

ADÈLE: Yes, your absence will cast a pall over the ball—go Marie, go.

VICOMTESS: I promised Eugène to dance the first quadrille with him—but with him, as soon as I am no longer bothered, the second begins. Listen dear Adèle—my friend, you cannot go in now. Get hold of yourself and I will be back soon to look for you. Then after all, think that, even though all the world abandons you—a good friend remains—a bit crazy—but at heart frank, and who knows that she's worth a hundred times less than you, but who loves you a hundred times more for all that—come, hug me, dry your beautiful eyes, swollen with tears and return quickly as to make all the women die of jealousy.

Bye! I'm going to watch so no one comes to bother you.

(she leaves; Anthony enters from a side door, hearing her last words and hangs back—Adèle doesn't see him)

ANTHONY: (watching the Vicomtess leave) She's a fair person, that woman.

(coming slowly before Adèle without being noticed. In anguish)

Oh! My God! My God!

ADÈLE: (sweetly and raising her head) I'm not angry with you, Anthony.

ANTHONY: Oh, you are an angel.

ADÈLE: I told you indeed nothing could hide from this society which surrounds us with all its coils, spies on us with all its eyes. You wanted me to come, and I came.

ANTHONY: Yes, you were insulted in a cowardly way—insulted—and as for me, I was here and I could do nothing for you because it was a woman who spoke—ten years of my life spent with you I would give for it to be a man who said what she said.

ADÈLE: But I haven't done anything to that woman—

ANTHONY: She at least rendered justice by retiring.

ADÈLE: Oh, but her poisoned words had already entered my heart and in that of the people who were here. From here you only hear the fracas of the music and the creaking of the floorboards. As for me, in the midst of all this, I hear the murmur of my name, my name repeated a hundred times, my name which belongs to another, my name which was given to me pure, and which I've returned to him soiled—it seems to me that all these words which buzz are only a phrase repeated by a hundred voices: "She's his mistress!"

ANTHONY: My friend! My Adèle!

ADÈLE: Then when I go back in—for I cannot remain here, they'll whisper, their eyes will devour my blushes, they will see the trace of my tears—and they will say "Ah, she wept—but he will comfort her—she's his mistress."

ANTHONY: Ah!

ADÈLE: The women will avoid me, the mothers will say to their daughters "Do you see that woman—she had an honorable husband—who loved her and made her happy. Nothing can excuse her sin. She's a woman one mustn't see—a ruined woman—she's his mistress."

ANTHONY: Oh, be quiet, be quiet! And among all these women what woman is more pure and more innocent than you? You fled! It as I who pursued you. I had no pity for your tears, it was I who ruined you—I who am a wretch, a coward—I dishonored you and can do nothing in reparation. Tell me what I must do for you—? Are there words which will comfort you? Demand my life, my blood—for mercy what do you want, what do you order?

ADÈLE: Nothing—you see, a frightful idea often comes to me. It's that perhaps, once, one single time, you might think in you heart "She gave in to me, she could give in to somebody else."

ANTHONY: I'd die instead.

ADÈLE: For you, too, I'd be a ruined woman. You too, you would say "She's my mistress!"

ANTHONY: Oh, no, no—you are my soul, my life, my love.

ADÈLE: Tell me, Anthony, if tomorrow I were free, would you still marry me?

ANTHONY: Oh, by God and by Honor, yes.

ADÈLE: Without fear? Without hesitation?

ANTHONY: With intoxication.

ADÈLE: Thanks! I still have God and you—what does the world matter to me? God and you know that a woman cannot resist so much love. These women are so vain, so proud, they would have succumbed as I did if my Anthony had loved them—best he didn't love them, right?

ANTHONY: Oh, no, no—

ADÈLE: For what woman could resist my Anthony? Ah—everything I've said is madness—I still want to be happy. I will forget everything so to remember only you. What do I care what the world will say? I won't see anyone—I will isolate myself with our love. You will stay near me. You will repeat every instant that you love, that you are happy, that we are happy. I will believe you—for I believe in your voice—in all that you tell me, when you speak everything inside me becomes quiet to listen, my heart no longer shakes, my face no longer burns, my tears stop, my remorse sleeps—I forget—!

ANTHONY: No—I will never leave you again, I take everything on myself—and may God punish me, yes, we will be happy yet—calm down.

ADÈLE: (in Anthony's arms) I am happy.

(the door opens from the salon and the Vicomtess appears)

Marie.

ANTHONY: Damnation!

(Adèle lets out a sob and escapes through a side door)

VICOMTESS: Sir, it was only after looking for you everywhere that I came here.

ANTHONY: (bitterly) And without doubt you had a very important reason.

VICOMTESS: Yes, sir, a man who calls himself your servant asks for you and insists on speaking only to you.

ANTHONY: A servant of mine? Who insists on speaking only to me? Oh, Madame, allow him to enter. If it is— and then—in the name of heaven—tell Adèle—tell the Baroness to come. Find her Madame—I beg you—you are her only friend.

VICOMTESS: I'm running—

(to Louis)

Enter.

ANTHONY: Louis! Oh, who brought you?

LOUIS: Colonel d'Hervey left Strasbourg yesterday morning. He will be here in a few hours.

ANTHONY: In a few hours?

(calling)

Adèle! Adèle!

VICOMTESS: (returning) She just left!

ANTHONY: To return home? Misfortune! Will I get there in time?

CURTAIN

ACT FIVE

A room in Adèle's home.

(a servant brings in torches and leaves; Adèle, entering, gives her boa to her chamber maid who follows her)

ADÈLE: You can go.

CHAMBERMAID: But Madame is going to remain alone?

ADÈLE: If I need you, I'll ring. Go.

(The maid goes.)

ADÈLE: (alone) Ah—here I am alone at last! I cannot

blush and cry alone. My God—what kind of fate is this that allows you to stretch your arm into the midst of the world, to seize on a woman who always had been virtuous, and who always desired to remain so, to drag her, despite her efforts and cries, breaking all the supports to which she clung, causing her ruin, her ruin, which would be the delight of another. The one whose salvation you desire more than all others? And you consent, oh, my God, that this woman be seen by the same eyes, pursued by the same insults as those who make a game of their dishonor? Oh, is this justice? One friend alone, alone in all the world, believes in my innocence and comforts me. There was too much joy and not enough shame. She finds me in his arms—abandoned! Ah, Anthony! Anthony—will you pursue me forever? Who's that?

ANTHONY: (entering) Adèle!

(with joy)

Ah!

ADÈLE: Oh, it's you again! You here in my husband's house—almost in the room of my daughter! Have pity on me! My servants still respect and honor me—do you want me to blush before my servants tomorrow?

ANTHONY: No one has seen me—anyway, I have to speak to you.

ADÈLE: Yes, you wanted to know if I was able to stand that frightful soirée—well, I am calm. I am peaceful—fear nothing. Retire.

ANTHONY: Oh, it's not that. Don't be alarmed by what I am going to tell you.

ADÈLE: Speak! Speak! What is it?

ANTHONY: You've got to come with me.

ADÈLE: You—and why?

ANTHONY: Why? Oh, my God! Poor Adèle—listen, you know that my life is yours, that I love you deliriously. Well, on my life, on my honor, you must come with me—instantly.

ADÈLE: Oh, my God—but what's wrong?

ANTHONY: If I told you "Adèle, the house next door is in flames, the walls burning, the stairway shaking, you must come with me," well, you'd have more time to waste.

(pulling her)

ADÈLE: Oh, you won't drag me again. Anthony, this is madness. Mercy! Mercy! Oh, I'll call, I'll shout.

ANTHONY: (releasing her) I must tell you everything, since you insist—well, courage, Adèle in an hour, your husband will be here.

ADÈLE: What is that you say?

ANTHONY: The Colonel is at the end of the street per-haps.

ADÈLE: This cannot be—this isn't the time for his return.

ANTHONY: If suspicions bring him here, if anonymous letters have been written?

ADÈLE: Suspicions, yes, yes—that's it. Oh, indeed, I am

lost. Save me—why haven't you decided something? You knew it before me—you've had time to think. Me, me—you see quite well my head is spinning.

ANTHONY: You have to undergo, first of all, an initial meeting.

ADÈLE: And then?

ANTHONY: And then we will take advice about every-thing—even of despair. If you were one of those virtu-ous women who made fun of you tonight, I would tell you, "Deceive him!"

ADÈLE: Oh, even if I were as false as that I couldn't de-ceive him for long—we are not unfortunate by half. Not us.

ANTHONY: Well, you see there's little hope to expect help from heaven by remaining here. Listen, I am free—every where I go my fortune follows me. Then, even if it failed me I could easily supplement it.

A carriage is below—listen, I've considered—there is no other way—if a devoted heart, if the whole life of a man is thrown at your feet—is enough for you—say yes—Italy, England, Germany, offer us asylum. I will tear you from your family, from your country. Well, I will be your family, and your country for you.

By changing our name, no one will know who we are during our life. No one will know who we are after our death. We will live isolated, you will be my wealth, my God, my life—I will have no other will than yours—no other joy than yours. Come, come, and we will forget the others so as only to remember ourselves.

ADÈLE: Yes, yes—well, a word to Clara.

ANTHONY: We don't have a minute to lose.

ADÈLE: My daughter—I have to kiss my daughter. You see it's a last goodbye—one eternal goodbye.

ANTHONY: Yes, yes, go, go—

(pushing her)

ADÈLE: Oh, my God!

ANTHONY: What's wrong with you then?

ADÈLE: My daughter, leave my daughter—who will ask an account one day of her mother's fault—who will live, perhaps, but no longer live for her. My daughter! Poor child—who will think she's presenting herself pure and innocent to the world but actually presents herself dishonored—like her mother, by her mother.

ANTHONY: Oh! My God!

ADÈLE: Isn't it true? A stain once fallen on a name can never be effaced. It hollows it, it gnaws it, it devours it. Oh, my daughter—my daughter—!

ANTHONY: Well, take her. Let her come with us! Even yesterday, I wouldn't have thought myself capable of loving her. The child of another and of you—well, she will be my daughter, my cherished child. I will love her like my own. But take her and let's leave. Take her now—each moment ruins you. What are you thinking about? He's going to come. He's coming. He's here!

ADÈLE: Oh unhappy me—what have I come to? Where have you led me? And it only took three months for this? A man confides his name to me—places his happiness in me. His daughter! He adores her! She's the hope of his old age. The being through whom he must survive.

You came three months ago. The spark of my love rekindled, I soiled the name he confided in me. I broke the happiness reposed on me—and that's not all there is. No that's not enough. I will run off with the child of his heart, I will deprive him in his old age of the caresses of his daughter and in exchange for his love I will return shame—ill fortune and abandonment. Do you know, Anthony, that this is infamous?

ANTHONY: Then what is to be done?

ADÈLE: Stay.

ANTHONY: And when he discovers everything?

ADÈLE: He will kill me.

ANTHONY: Kill you? Him, kill you? You, die? Me, ruin you? That's impossible—aren't you afraid to die?

ADÈLE: Oh, no—it reunites.

ANTHONY: It separates. Do you think that I believe in

your dreams and that for them, I am going to risk what remains to me of life and joy? You want to die, well, listen, I too want that. But I don't want to die alone, you see I will be jealous of the tomb that shuts you in. Blessed be God who gave me an isolated life that I can quit without costing tears in beloved eyes—blessed be God who allowed that from the age of hope I had exhausted everything and was tired of everything—a single thread attached me to this world—it is cut—and I too, I want to die—but with you. I want the last beatings of our hearts to answer each other, that our last sighs be mixed. Do you understand? A sweet death, like sleep— a death happier than our life. Then who knows? From pity perhaps they will throw our bodies in the same tomb.

ADÈLE: Oh, yes, this death with you—eternity in your arms—oh, that will be heaven, if my memory could die with me. But do you understand, Anthony? That memory, will remain living in the heart of all who knew us. They'll demand a reckoning for my daughter of my life and my death. They'll tell her, "Your mother, she thought that a name already stained could be cleansed with blood. Child, your mother was deceived. Her name is still dishonored—branded, and you, you will bear the name of your mother."

They will tell her, "She thought to flee shame in death and she died in the arms of the man to whom she owed her shame."

And if she tries to deny it, they will raise the slab on our tomb and say to her, "Look, there they are."

ANTHONY: Oh, are we cursed then? Not to be able to live or to die, even?

ADÈLE: Yes, yes—I must die alone. You see—you are ruining me by being here without hope of saving me. You can do only one thing for me. Go away! In the name of heaven, go away!

ANTHONY: Me—go away! Leave you—when he's going to come? To have you taken away and lose you again. Hell! And if he doesn't kill you? If he forgives you? Having, in order to possess you, committed rape, violence, and adultery, why hesitate at a new crime to keep you? To lose my soul for so little? Satan is laughing—you are mad. No, no, you belong to me as man belongs to misfortune.

(taking her in his arms)

You must live for me. I will carry you off. Bad luck to anyone who tries to stop me.

ADÈLE: Oh—oh!

ANTHONY: Shout and cry—no matter!

ADÈLE: My child. My child!

ANTHONY: She's a child. Tomorrow she will laugh.

(They are getting ready to leave. Two blows of a hammer are heard on the coachman's door.)

ADÈLE: (escaping from his arms) Ah, it's him, oh, my God, my God, have pity on me—pardon, pardon!

ANTHONY: (leaving her) Come— everything's done.

ADÈLE: He's coming up the stairs. They are ringing— it's him—flee! Flee!

ANTHONY: (locking the door) Eh—As for me, I don't wish to flee. Listen, you said just now that you weren't afraid to die?

ADÈLE: No, no—oh kill me, for mercy!

ANTHONY: A death which would save your reputation and that of your child?

ADÈLE: I demand it on my knees.

A VOICE: (outside) Open! Open! Force the door!

ANTHONY: With your last breath you won't hate your murderer?

ADÈLE: I will bless him—but hurry up! That door.

ANTHONY: Don't be afraid. Death will be here before him. But think of it, death.

ADÈLE: I demand it, I insist upon it, I beg it.

(hurling herself into his arms)

I am coming to get it.

ANTHONY: (giving her a kiss) Well, die.

ADÈLE: (falling in a chair) Ah!

(At the same moment the door is beaten in. Colonel d'Hervey rushes on stage, followed by several servants.)

COLONEL: Infamous! What do I see? Adèle—dead.

ANTHONY: Yes, dead! She resisted me and I murdered her!

(He throws his dagger at the Colonel's feet.)

CURTAIN

ABOUT ALEXANDRE DUMAS PÈRE

ALEXANDER DUMAS PÈRE was born in 1802, the son of a Napoleonic general. He began his writing career as a playwright, penning such popular pieces as *Henri III et sa Cour* (1829), *Richard Darlington* (1831), *Kean* (1836), and *Mademoiselle de Belle-Isle* (1839). By the early 1840s he was churning out the wonderful historical romances for which he's best known today, including *Le Comte de Monte Cristo* (1844) and *Les Trois Mousquetaires* (1844). He died in 1870. His son, Alexandre Dumas Fils (1824-1895), was also a well-known playwright.

ABOUT FRANK J. MORLOCK

FRANK J. MORLOCK has written and translated many plays since retiring from the legal profession in 1992. His translations have also appeared on Project Gutenberg, the Alexandre Dumas Père web page, Literature in the Age of Napoléon, Infinite Artistries.com, and Munsey's (formerly Blackmask). In 2006 he received an award from the North American Jules Verne Society for his translations of Verne's plays. He lives and works in Maryland.

www.ingramcontent.com/pod-product-compliance
Lightning Source LLC
LaVergne TN
LVHW011205080426
835508LV00007B/614